PARTITION

OF THE

REAL ESTATE

OF

THE LATE GEORGE ODIN.

BOSTON:
PRESS OF GEO. C. RAND & AVERY, 3 CORNHILL.
1868.

To the Honorable the Judge of the Probate Court in and for the County of Suffolk:

Pursuant to your warrant to us directed, dated Aug. 24, A.D. 1868, and authorizing us to make the partition hereinafter set forth, we, the Commissioners therein named, were first sworn, to wit, on Sept. 2, A.D. 1868, to faithfully and impartially execute the duties assigned us by said warrant, as appears by a certificate of such oath made on said warrant by the person who administered it; and we gave sufficient notice to all persons interested of the time and place appointed by us for making the partition by said warrant directed, that they might be present at the making thereof,—there being no heir-at-law or devisee absent from the State, requiring the appointment of an agent by the Court. Such notice was also given by us in the Boston Daily Advertiser, a newspaper printed in the County of Suffolk, on the tenth, seventeenth, and twenty first days of September last, as appears by the following, which is a true copy of one of said notices, viz.:—

COMMONWEALTH OF MASSACHUSETTS.

SUFFOLK, ss.

To all parties interested in any of the real estate of George Odin, late of Boston, in said county, deceased, testate:

The undersigned, appointed by the Probate Court for said County, Commissioners to make partition of all the real estate of said deceased, not specifically devised, lying in this State, among the devisees in remainder, hereby notify you to appear at a meeting to be held at the office of C. U. Cotting, No. 9 Tremont Street, Boston, on Tuesday, the thirteenth day of October next, at three and a half o'clock in the afternoon, when and where said Commissioners will proceed to make said partition; and you are hereby notified, that you may be present at the making thereof.

In witness whereof we have hereto set our hands this second day of September, in the year eighteen hundred and sixty-eight.

JOHN H. THORNDIKE,
NATH'L J. BRADLEE,
CHAS. U. COTTING, } Commissioners.

At the time and place mentioned in the foregoing copy of said notice, we met for the performance of the duties assigned us by said warrant; and all the parties interested were present, either in person or by their agents or attorneys, as follows, viz.:—

Harriet W. O. Kellogg, by George A. Kettell, her agent; William H. Webb, as trustee for Benjamin Dalton Dorr, said Benjamin Dalton Dorr, Mary W. D. Schaffer, Esther O. D. Webb, and Harriet O. Carpenter, all by William Gaston, Harvey Jewell, and J. Edward Carpenter, their attorneys; George O. Currier for himself; George O. Currier and Charles H. Richardson, trustees for Amelia O. Richardson, and said Amelia O. Richardson, all by said George O. Currier; Mary L. Currier by George O. Currier, her agent; Harriet W. Currier by Benjamin H. Currier, her guardian; Anna F. Odin by Edward Blake, Esq., her attorney, and Harriet L. Odin by John L. Emmons, her guardian.

And we appraised all the real estate lying in this State, of which GEORGE ODIN, late of said Boston, in said county, deceased, died seized, not specifically devised by the will of said deceased, and which was required to be included in said partition, as follows: —

1. All that lot of land in said Boston, with the buildings thereon, bounded north-west by High Street ninety feet five inches; north-east by land now or late of John Grew, one hundred and twenty feet; south-east by Purchase Street seventy-eight feet eight inches; south-west by brick house and land, now or late of Dow and Loring, fifty-nine feet six and a half inches; south-east by the same six feet eight inches, and south-west by land late of Mary Turner, by a line passing through the middle of the partition wall, about thirty-eight feet, be said measures more or less; and being the premises conveyed to the said Odin by deeds recorded with Suffolk Deeds, lib. 621, fol. 291; lib. 853, fol. 56; lib. 854, fol. 85; lib. 854, fol. 85; lib. 854, fol. 270; lib. 647, fol. 68, fol. 69, and fol. 70; lib. 561, fol. 203; lib. 563, fol. 116 and fol. 117; and lib. 573, fol. 14, with and subject to all the rights, easements, and reservations in said deeds, or either of them, referred to.

And we have divided the foregoing lot into three several parcels for appraisal, upon the following terms; viz., All assessments for "betterments," so called, are to be paid by the respective parties to whom the estates are assigned and set off by this partition. All rights of passage-way, drainage, or suction, as between said three several parcels, are hereby extinguished, and are to remain as they now are by sufferance only. The partition-walls on either side of the middle of said three several parcels shall be built on the dividing lines between said several parcels, one-half on each parcel; and shall be suitable for first-class wholesale stores. And the party first building shall receive from his neighbor and abuttor, at the time he makes use of the same, one-half part of the reasonable cost at such time of so much thereof as he shall then use.

Subject to these provisions, we sever and appraise said foregoing lot extending from High Street to Purchase Street, as follows; viz., —

Lot A. All that parcel of land in said Boston, with the buildings thereon, bounded north-west by High Street twenty-six feet ten and two-thirds inches; north-east by land late of John Grew, since of Eben B. Phillips, one hundred and twenty feet; south-east by Purchase Street twenty-six feet, and south-west by the parcel of land next hereinafter described and appraised, by a line to pass through the middle of the partition-wall as above provided for, one hundred and thirteen feet, — containing $3{,}027\frac{11}{12}$ square feet, — with the benefit of an unrecorded agreement made June 18, 1868, by said Phillips with the devisees of said Odin, to sell and convey a strip of land eight inches in width, on the north-east boundary of the above-described parcel, for eight dollars per square foot, and interest, and the wall thereon for $1,958.00 and interest, within one year; but upon the conditions therein mentioned: and we appraise said parcel of land and buildings at the sum of thirty thousand two hundred and seventy-nine dollars and seventeen cents.

Lot B. All that parcel of land in said Boston, with the buildings thereon, bounded north-west by High Street twenty-six feet ten and two-thirds inches; north-east by the parcel of land next hereinbefore described and appraised, by a line to pass through the middle of the partition-wall, as above provided for, one hundred and thirteen feet; south-east by Purchase Street twenty-six feet, and south-west by the parcel of land next hereinafter described and appraised, by a line to pass through the middle of the partition-wall, as above provided for, one hundred and six feet and one inch, — containing 2,848$\frac{1}{12}$ square feet: and we appraise this last-described parcel of land and buildings at the sum of twenty-eight thousand four hundred and eighty dollars and eighty-three cents.

Lot C. All that parcel of land in said Boston, with the buildings thereon, bounded north-west by High Street thirty-six feet four and two-thirds inches; north-east by the parcel of land next hereinbefore described and appraised, by a line to pass through the middle of the partition-wall, as above provided for, one hundred and six feet and one inch; south-east by Purchase Street twenty-six feet eleven and a half inches; south-west by land now or late of Dow and Loring, by a line passing through the middle of a brick partition-wall, fifty-nine feet eight inches; south-east by the same six feet ten inches, and south-west by land late of Mary Turner, by a line passing through the middle of the partition-wall, thirty-eight feet, — containing 3,123½ square feet: and we appraise this last-described parcel of land and buildings at the sum of thirty-one thousand two hundred and thirty-five dollars.

Number 2. We next appraised all that lot of land in said Boston, with the buildings thereon, bounded north-west by High Street twenty-six feet nine inches; north-east by land late of Tileston, forty-eight feet nine inches; south-east by land late of John B. Andrews twenty-six feet six inches, and south-west by land late of Aaron Hill forty-nine feet and two inches; all said boundary lines, except upon the street, passing through the middle of brick walls. Said lot contains 1,299½ square feet, and is the same conveyed to said Odin by John Homans, by deed dated May 5, 1849, and recorded with Suffolk Deeds, lib. 600, fol. 56, subject to the reservation therein mentioned: and we appraise the same at the sum of fourteen thousand two hundred and ninety-four dollars and fifty cents.

Number 3. We next appraised that lot of land in said Boston, with the buildings thereon, bounded easterly by Suffolk Street, twenty-three feet; northerly, by land now, or late, of Joseph W. Parlin, and of Joseph Colby, forty-six feet; westerly, by land now, or late, of James Hendley, twenty-three feet; and southerly, by land now, or late, of Moses Standish, forty-six feet; containing 1,058 square feet, and being the same premises conveyed to said Odin by Henry W. Walker, by deed dated Feb. 6, 1865, and recorded with Suffolk Deeds, lib. 854, fol. 47: and we appraise the same at the sum of four thousand dollars.

Number 4. We next appraised that lot of land in said Boston, with the buildings thereon, bounded northerly by Castle Street, twenty feet; westerly, by land late of William Gardiner, fifty-eight feet nine inches; southerly, by the same, ten feet four inches; easterly, by land late of John French, fourteen feet four inches; southerly, again by the same, ten feet three inches; and easterly, by a ten-feet passage-way, forty-three feet seven inches; containing 1,021½ square feet, and being the same premises conveyed to said Odin by Maria E. Winslow and another, by deed dated May 19, 1864, and recorded with Suffolk Deeds, lib. 843, fol. 165, with all the rights thereto belonging; and we appraise the same at the sum of four thousand five hundred dollars.

Number 5. We next appraised that lot of land in said Boston, with the buildings thereon, bounded north-easterly by Pleasant Street, forty-nine feet seven inches; south-easterly, by land late of Timothy Tileston, forty-seven feet nine inches; south-westerly, by land late of John Spear and others, forty-seven feet ten inches; and north-westerly, by land late of Clark Parker, sixty-five feet, or however otherwise bounded, measured, or described; and being the same premises conveyed to said Odin by George Parkman, by deed dated May 17, 1836, and recorded with Suffolk Deeds, lib. 405, fol. 114: and we appraise the same at the sum of ten thousand nine hundred and twenty-eight dollars and thirty cents.

Number 6. We next appraised that lot of land in said Boston, with the buildings thereon, bounded westerly by Carver Street, nineteen feet three inches; northerly, by land now, or late, of Smith & Weeks, by a line passing through the middle of the partition-wall, thirty-two feet two inches; easterly, by land late of Williams, five feet two inches; northerly, by the same, four inches, easterly again, by the same, fourteen feet one inch; and southerly, by land late of James Standish, by a line passing through the middle of the partition-wall, thirty-two feet ten and a half inches; being the same premises conveyed to said Odin by Samuel F. Towle, by deed dated September, 1863, and recorded with Suffolk Deeds, lib. 832, fol. 201: and we appraise the same at the sum of six thousand dollars.

Number 7. We next appraised that lot of land in said Boston, with the buildings thereon, bounded southerly by Harvard Street, twenty feet; easterly, by land late of David Ellis, sixty-one feet four inches; northerly, by the end of Kneeland Place, eighteen feet; north-westerly, by land late of Josiah Knapp, five feet two inches; and westerly, by the same, fifty-six feet four inches; containing about 1221 square feet, and being the same premises conveyed to said Odin by John O. Pettes, by deed dated Oct. 17, 1853, and recorded with Suffolk Deeds, lib. 653, fol. 195: and we appraise the same at the sum of ten thousand dollars.

Number 8. We next appraised that lot of land in said Boston, with the dwelling-house thereon, numbered five (5), bounded easterly by Kneeland Place, twenty feet; northerly, by land and house numbered four (4), formerly of Abijah S. Johnson, by a line passing through the middle of the partition-wall, sixty feet; westerly, by land late of Josiah Stedman, twenty feet; and southerly, by land and house numbered six (6), formerly of said Johnson, by a line passing through the middle of the partition-wall, sixty feet; being the same premises to which said Odin derived title under two mortgages; one dated March 15, 1855, and recorded with Suffolk Deeds, lib. 677, fol. 135, and the other dated Nov. 30, 1859, and recorded in lib. 768, fol. 271, subject to the easements and agreements therein mentioned: and we appraise the same at the sum of six thousand five hundred dollars.

Number 9. We next appraised that lot of land in said Boston, with the buildings thereon, bounded south-east by Chauncy Street, twenty-one feet; south-west, by a line passing through the middle of a brick partition-wall, fifty-seven feet six inches (said line being, on said street, twelve feet and nine inches distant from the north-east corner of land late of J. W. Bradlee); westerly, in the rear, twenty-four feet ten inches; and north-easterly, by a line passing through the middle of a brick partition-wall, seventy feet and eleven inches to the first boundary on said street; being the same premises conveyed to said Odin by William A. Swift, et al., by deed dated Dec. 1, 1845, and recorded with Suffolk Deeds, lib. 553, fol. 279; reference being had thereto for more particular description, with and subject to all the rights and easements now lawfully used, enjoyed, or connected therewith: and we appraise the same at the sum of eighteen thousand dollars.

Number 10. We next appraised that lot of land in said Boston, with the buildings thereon, bounded easterly by Wendell Street, seventeen feet eight inches; northerly, by land now, or late, of Bancroft, by a line passing through the middle of the partition-wall, fifty-two feet; westerly, by a four-feet passage-way, seventeen feet eight inches; and southerly, by land late of Benjamin Crombie, by a line passing through the middle of the partition-wall, fifty-one feet; being the same premises conveyed to said Odin by Robert Briggs, by deed dated Nov. 23, 1835, and recorded with Suffolk Deeds, lib. 399, fol. 210, with all the rights and easements, as in said deed referred to: and we appraise the same at the sum of three thousand dollars.

Number 11. We next appraised that lot of land in said Boston, with the buildings thereon, bounded westerly by Broad Street, twenty feet; northerly, by land late of Uriah Cotting, forty-four feet; easterly, by land late of the Broad-Street Association, thirteen feet, and by a strip of land, or passage-way for light and air, seven feet; and southerly, by land late of Ward N. Boylston, forty feet; being the same premises conveyed to said Odin by Nabby Joy, by deed dated Oct. 10, 1836, and recorded with Suffolk Deeds, lib. 411, fol. 106, subject to the conditions in said deed, and also subject to a lease of part of said premises to Bartlett, Smith, & Co., to July 1, A. D. 1869: and we appraise said premises at the sum of fifteen thousand dollars.

Number 12. We next appraised that lot of land in said Boston, with the buildings thereon, bounded easterly by Broad Street, twenty-two feet; northerly, by a brick store and land late of Samuel Sanford, forty feet; westerly, on the rear, twenty-two feet; and southerly, by a brick store and land late of Samuel Appleton, forty feet, with the privilege of erecting buildings, and placing joists or timbers, as set forth in the deed from Samuel Sanford to said Odin, of said premises, dated Feb. 12, 1830, and recorded with Suffolk Deeds, lib. 344, fol. 153; reference being had thereto for particulars: and we appraise the same at the sum of eighteen thousand six hundred and seventy-one dollars and seventy-eight cents.

13. We next viewed a lot of land in said Boston, with the buildings thereon, bounded northerly by Pinckney Street, fifty feet six inches; easterly by land late of John H. Belcher, since of Lyman Nichols, by land late of Stephen Higginson, since of Brown, and by a passage-way extending to Joy Street, forty-three feet four inches; southerly, by said passage-way, five feet seven inches; easterly, by the same, three feet; southerly, again, by land conveyed by said Odin to Thomas B. Curtis, and by land late of Lemuel Shaw, forty-three feet; and westerly by land late of Stephen Higginson, since of Stevens, fifty-three feet, be said measures more or less. For the title of said Odin, see deed of George Parker to him, dated May 26, 1824, and recorded with Suffolk Deeds, lib. 291, fol. 7; deed of Higginson to him dated Oct. 22, 1828, and recorded lib. 331, fol. 242, &c.; deed of Higginson to him dated April 28, 1831, and recorded lib. 352, fol. 184; and deed of Higginson to him dated June 29, 1831, and recorded lib. 353, fol. 152; with all the rights and easements belonging, and with and subject to the easements and agreements mentioned or referred to in an indenture dated Aug. 5, 1837, and recorded lib. 423, fol. 71, and in another indenture dated June 5, 1846, and recorded lib. 568, fol. 48.

And we have divided the foregoing lot into two several parcels for appraisal as follows: —

Lot D. All that parcel of land in said Boston, with the buildings thereon, bounded northerly by Pinckney Street twenty-nine feet one and a half inches; easterly by land of Lyman Nichols, by land of Brown, and by a passage-way extending to Joy Street, forty-three feet four inches; southerly by said passage-way, five feet seven inches; easterly by the same three feet; southerly by land conveyed by said Odin to Thomas B. Curtis, twenty-two feet ten and a half inches; and westerly by the parcel of land next hereinafter described, by a line passing through the middle of the partition-wall fifty-one feet ten and three-quarters inches; with and subject to the easements and agreements above referred to. All existing easements of drainage, if any, over and through the lot next hereinafter described, shall wholly cease after Aug. 1, 1869: and we appraise this last-described parcel of land and buildings at the sum of eight thousand five hundred dollars.

Lot E. All that parcel of land in said Boston, with the buildings thereon, bounded northerly by Pinckney Street twenty-one feet four and a half inches; easterly by the parcel of land next hereinbefore described, by a line passing through the middle of the partition-wall fifty-one feet ten and three-quarters inches; southerly by land now or late of Thomas B. Curtis, and by land late of Lemuel Shaw, twenty-two feet two inches, and westerly by land late of Stephen Higginson, since of Stevens, fifty-three feet four and a half inches. All existing easements of drainage, if any, over and through the lot next hereinbefore described, shall wholly cease after Aug. 1, 1869; subject to a lease to Charles F. Small, which will expire April 1, 1869: and we appraise this last-described parcel of land and buildings at the sum of seven thousand dollars.

14. We next viewed a large lot of land in said Boston, with the buildings thereon, bounded northerly by Howard Street eighty-three feet, westerly by Bulfinch Street one hundred and fifty-nine feet four inches, southerly by land late of David Gould, trustee, since of Brigham, twenty-nine feet five inches, easterly by land of Dixwell twenty-four feet ten inches, southerly by the same thirty feet eight inches, easterly by the end of a passage-way, by land hereinafter described (which was conveyed to said Odin by James Dennie), and by land now or late of Winchester, fifty-eight feet four inches, southerly by land now or late of Winchester eighteen feet seven and a half inches, easterly by land now or late of Samuel Hammond fifteen feet two inches, southerly by the same one foot six inches, easterly by the same twenty-one feet six inches, southerly again by the same one foot eight inches, and easterly again by the same, by a line passing through the middle of the partition-wall forty-two feet eight inches to the first boundary on Howard Street, be said measures, however, more or less. For the title of said Odin see deed of Francis Southack to him, dated May 14, 1818, recorded with Suffolk Deeds, lib. 258, fol. 130; deed of William F. Brazer to him, dated Nov. 24, 1818, recorded lib. 260, fol. 107; deed of said Southack to him, dated March 28, 1823, and recorded lib. 282, fol. 79, &c.; deed of Samuel Hammond to him, dated June 24, 1825, and recorded lib. 301, fol. 137, 138, and deeds of David Gould, trustee, and others to him, dated Oct. 10, 1844, and recorded lib. 532, fol. 14 and 16; subject, however, to the agreements and provisions in said deed of said Hammond, and also subject to the easements and agreements in the deed of said Odin to said Hammond, dated June 25, 1825, and recorded lib. 301, fol. 141.

And we have divided the foregoing lot into seven several parcels for appraisal upon the terms and stipulations hereinafter set forth respectively as follows: —

Lot F. All that parcel of land in said Boston, with the buildings thereon, bounded northerly by Howard Street twenty-one feet seven inches, easterly by land now or late of Samuel Hammond, by a line passing through the middle of the partition-wall forty-two feet, southerly by the same one foot two inches, easterly by the same twenty-one feet six inches, southerly by the same one foot six inches, easterly again by the same fifteen feet two inches, southerly by land now or late of Winchester eighteen feet eight inches, and westerly by land hereinafter described by a line passing through the middle of the partition-wall seventy-nine feet and eight inches to the first boundary on said Howard Street, with and subject to the easements, agreements, and provisions hereinbefore mentioned and referred to. This parcel of land is subject to a right and easement in the privy in the rear or southerly part thereof as an appurtenance to Lot J, hereinafter described, until Aug. 1, 1869, but no longer; and is to have no right of way or drainage whatsoever over the estates next westerly thereof after said Aug. 1, 1869: and we appraise said parcel of land, subject as aforesaid, at the sum of ten thousand dollars.

Lot G. All that parcel of land in said Boston, with the buildings thereon, bounded westerly by Bulfinch Street sixteen feet two and a half inches, north-westerly by the junction of Bulfinch Street and Howard Street ten feet nine inches, northerly by Howard Street fifty feet eight and a quarter inches, easterly by the parcel of land next hereinbefore described, by a line passing through the middle of the partition-wall twenty feet two inches, and southerly by the parcel of land next hereinafter described, on one line measuring twenty-one feet eight inches, and on another (through the middle of the partition-wall) thirty-six feet two and a half inches; subject, always however, to a right of way and drainage in common with the proprietors of lots H, I, and J (hereinafter described) in a passage-way as now laid out over and across the rear or easterly end of said parcel of land, which way and drain are to be maintained at the joint expense of said four several parcels, and subject to the easements as granted above to Lot F until Aug. 1, 1869. All other existing easements of drainage, if any, over this lot (as between Lots G, H, I, and J, herein described), are to wholly cease after said Aug. 1, 1869: and we appraise this parcel of land subject as aforesaid, at the sum of twelve thousand five hundred dollars.

Lot H. All that parcel of land in said Boston, with the buildings thereon, bounded westerly by Bulfinch Street, twenty-two feet six inches; northerly by the parcel of land next hereinbefore described, on one line passing through the middle of the partition-wall thirty-six feet two and a half inches, and on another line, measuring twenty-one feet eight inches; easterly by the parcel of land designated F, and hereinbefore described, by a line passing through the middle of the partition-wall twenty-one feet four inches, and southerly by the parcel of land next hereinafter described, by a line passing through the middle of the partition-wall fifty-seven feet; with and subject to a right of way and drainage in common with the proprietors of lots G, I, and J (herein described) in the passage-way to Howard Street, as now laid out over and across the rear or easterly end of this parcel of land; which way and drain are to be maintained at the joint expense of said four several parcels; and subject to the easements as above granted to lot F, until Aug. 1, 1869. All other existing easements of drainage, if any, over this lot (as between lots G, H, I, and J, herein described), are to wholly cease after said Aug. 1, 1869: and we appraise this parcel of land at the sum of ten thousand dollars.

Lot I. All that parcel of land in said Boston, with the buildings thereon, bounded westerly by Bulfinch Street, twenty-three feet and three-quarters of an inch; northerly by said street, and by the parcel of land next hereinbefore described, by a line passing through the middle of the partition-wall, fifty-nine feet eight and three-quarters inches; easterly by the parcel of land designated F, and hereinbefore described, by a line passing through the middle of the partition-wall, twenty-two feet six inches, and southerly by the parcel of land next hereinafter described, by a line passing through the middle of the partition, fifty-eight feet seven and a half inches; with and subject to a right of way and drainage in common with the proprietors of lots G, H, and J (herein described) in the passage-way to Howard Street, as now laid out over and across the rear or easterly end of this parcel of land, which way and drain are to be maintained at the joint expense of said four several parcels, and subject to the easements as above granted to lot F, until Aug. 1, 1869. All other existing easements of drainage, if any, over this lot (as between lots G, H, I, and J, herein described), are to wholly cease after said Aug. 1, 1869: and we appraise this parcel of land at the sum of nine thousand five hundred dollars.

Lot J. All that parcel of land in said Boston, with the buildings thereon, bounded westerly by Bulfinch Street, twenty-two feet eleven inches; northerly by the parcel of land next hereinbefore described, by a line passing through the middle of the partition, fifty-eight feet seven and a half inches; easterly by the parcel of land above designated as F, and by land now or late of Winchester, twenty-one feet one inch; southerly, by the parcel of land next hereinafter described, by a line passing through the middle of the partition-wall, fifteen feet five inches; easterly by the same, one foot ten inches; and southerly by the same, by a line passing through the middle of the partition-wall, forty-two feet three inches; with a right of way and drainage in common with the proprietors of lots G, H, and I (herein described) in the passage-way to Howard Street, as now laid out over and across the rears or easterly ends of said lots, G, H, and I, which way and drain are to be maintained at the joint expense of said four several parcels; subject to the easements above granted lot F, until Aug. 1. 1869. All other existing easements of drainage, if any, over this lot (as between lots G, H, I, and J, herein described), are to wholly cease after said Aug. 1, 1869. Also with a right and easement in the privy in the rear or southerly part of the lot designated as F, hereinbefore described, until Aug. 1, 1869, but no longer; subject, however, to the privilege of light and air, as appurtenant to the estate next hereinafter described, until Aug. 1, 1874, but no longer: and we appraise this parcel of land at the sum of nine thousand dollars.

Lot K. All that parcel of land in said Boston, with the buildings thereon, bounded westerly by Bulfinch Street forty-five feet eight inches; northerly by the parcel of land next hereinbefore described, by a line passing through the middle of the partition-wall forty-two feet three inches; westerly, by the same, one foot ten inches; northerly, by the same, by a line passing through the middle of the partition-wall, fifteen feet five inches; easterly by land now or late of Winchester, and by land conveyed to said Odin by James Dennie, forty-six feet five and a half inches; and southerly by the parcel of land next hereinafter described, by a line passing through the middle of the partition-wall, fifty-eight feet six and a half inches; with a privilege of light and air over the rear of the parcel of land next hereinbefore described, until Aug. 1, 1874, but no longer, and subject to a lease to Lucy A. Bailey, which will expire Aug. 1, 1874. And all existing easements of drainage over any adjoining estate herein described shall wholly cease after Aug. 1, 1874: and we appraise this parcel of land, subject as aforesaid, at the sum of seventeen thousand dollars.

Lot L. All that parcel of land in said Boston, with the buildings thereon, bounded westerly by Bulfinch Street, thirty-one feet ten inches; northerly, by the parcel of land next hereinbefore described, by a line passing through the middle of the partition-wall, fifty-eight feet six and a half inches; easterly by land conveyed to said Odin by James Dennie, and by the end of a passage-way extending to Somerset Street, eight feet six inches; southerly, by land now, or late, of Dixwell, thirty feet five inches; easterly, by the same, twenty-four feet eight inches, and southerly by land now, or late, of Brigham, thirty feet. The rear part of said parcel is subject to the aforesaid lease to Lucy A. Bailey, which will expire Aug. 1, 1874. And all existing easements of drainage over any adjoining estate herein described shall wholly cease after Aug. 1, 1869. Subject, furthermore, to a lease to Sarah A. White, which will expire Sept. 1, 1869: and we appraise this parcel of land at the sum of ten thousand dollars.

Number 15. We next appraised that lot of land in said Boston, with the buildings thereon, bounded easterly by Somerset Street, twenty-five feet; northerly by land now, or late, of Winchester, by a line passing through the middle of the partition-wall, ninety-five feet; westerly by lots above designated as K and L, twenty-five feet, and southerly by a ten-feet passage-way ninety-five feet; be said measures more or less. Being the same premises conveyed to said Odin by James Dennie, by deed dated July 25, 1856, and recorded with Suffolk Deeds, lib. 702, fol. 188; with the rights and easements thereto belonging; but all existing easements of drainage over any of the adjoining estate hereinbefore described shall wholly cease after Aug. 1, 1869. The outbuildings, with other privileges, on the rear of these premises, now used and occupied by Lucy A. Bailey, are subject to her tenancy therein, as the same may lawfully appear: and we appraise this lot at the sum of sixteen thousand five hundred dollars.

Number 16. We next appraised that lot of land in said Boston, with the buildings thereon, bounded easterly by Bulfinch Street, twenty-two feet four inches; northerly by a four-feet passage-way sixty-seven feet eight inches; westerly by land now or late of Thompson, twenty. two feet four inches; and southerly by land now or late of Thomas Crehore, by a line passing through the middle of the partition-wall, about sixty-six feet; being the same premises conveyed to said Odin by Thomas Crehore, by deed dated Jan. 31, 1845, and recorded with Suffolk Deeds, lib. 538, fol. 21. Subject however, to the reservation of passage-way as therein set forth: and we appraise this lot at the sum of eleven thousand dollars.

Number 17. We next appraised that lot of land in said Boston, with the buildings thereon, bounded southerly by McLean Street, twenty-four feet six inches; easterly by the house and land next hereinafter described, by a line passing through the middle of the partition-wall fifty-six feet; northerly by land late of Bosworth, twenty-four feet six inches; and westerly by land late of Mary J. Turner, fifty-six feet; with and subject to all the easements belonging and referred to in Asa Clark's deed to said Odin of said lot, dated July 3, 1824, and recorded with Suffolk Deeds, lib. 291, fol. 203: but all existing easements of drainage, dominant or servient, connected with the two lots of land next hereinafter described, are to wholly cease after Aug. 1, 1869: and we appraise this lot at the sum of eight thousand dollars.

Number 18. We next appraised that lot of land in said Boston, with the buildings thereon, bounded southerly by McLean Street, twenty-four feet six inches; westerly by the house and land next hereinbefore described, by a line passing through the middle of the partition-wall fifty-six feet; northerly by the lot of land next hereinafter described, twenty-four feet six inches; and easterly by house and land late of Jaquith, fifty-five feet; with and subject to all the easements belonging and referred to in Asa Clark's deed to said Odin, dated Jan. 21, 1824, and recorded with Suffolk Deeds, lib. 288, fol. 74: but all existing easements of drainage, dominant or servient, connected with the lot of land next hereinbefore described and the lot of land next hereinafter described, are to wholly cease after Aug. 1, 1869: and we appraise this lot at the sum of eight thousand five hundred dollars.

Number 19. We next appraised that lot of land in said Boston, with the buildings thereon, bounded northerly by Allen Street, twenty-four feet six inches; easterly by land of Jaquith, by a line passing through the middle of the partition-wall thirty-five feet; southerly by the lot of land next hereinbefore described, twenty-four feet six inches; and westerly by land late of Greenough, thirty-five feet; being the same premises conveyed to said Odin by Asa and Phineas Clark by deed dated Jan. 21, 1824, and recorded with Suffolk Deeds, lib. 288, fol. 61; with all the rights and easements belonging: but all existing easements of drainage, dominant or servient, connected with the two lots of land next hereinbefore described, are to wholly cease after Aug. 1, 1869: and we appraise this lot at the sum of five thousand five hundred dollars.

Number 20. We next appraised that parcel of land in Chelsea, in said county of Suffolk, with the buildings thereon, bounded easterly by the Old County Road, fifty-six feet; south-easterly by Pearl Street, twenty feet; south-westerly by lot fifty-four (54), Pearl Street, so called, eighty-one feet seven and a half inches; north-westerly by land devised to the wife of Samuel F. Towle by the said Odin, by a codicil to his will, fifty-nine feet eight and a quarter inches; and north-easterly by land now or late of Ezra Hawkes, fifty-seven feet six inches; be said measures more or less. For the title of said Odin see Ezra Hawkes's deed to him, dated Oct. 27, 1845, and recorded with Suffolk Deeds, lib. 552, fol. 202; James C. Nottage's deed to him, dated Oct. 25, 1845, and recorded lib. 552, fol. 203; and Hannah Young's deed to him, dated July 8, 1846, and recorded lib. 564, fol. 205: and we appraise the above-described parcel at the sum of five thousand dollars.

21. And we next viewed a lot of land in said Boston, with the buildings thereon, bounded southerly by the middle of Lyndeboro' Place, twenty-seven feet; easterly by land late of James Garland, forty-five feet ten inches; northerly by land late of Frederick Beck, twenty-seven feet; and westerly by land now or late of Brown, forty-six feet two and a half inches; being the same lot conveyed to said Odin by J. E. & N. Brown, by deed dated Sept. 4, 1837, and recorded with Suffolk Deeds, lib. 424, fol. 20. With and subject to all the rights, easements, and restrictions therein mentioned; subject also to the grant made by said Odin to said Browns, by deed dated Sept. 25, 1837, and recorded in lib. 424, fol. 271.

And we have divided the foregoing lot into two several parcels for appraisal upon the terms and stipulations hereinafter set forth: —

Lot M. All that lot of land in said Boston, with the buildings thereon, bounded southerly by the middle of Lyndeboro' Place, thirteen feet six and a half inches; easterly by land-late of James Garland, forty-five feet five and a half inches; northerly by land late of Frederick Beck, thirteen feet six inches; and westerly by the lot of land next hereinafter described, by a line passing through the middle of a covered common passage-way and the partition-wall over the same, as they now exist, forty-five feet five and three-quarters inches. With and subject to the rights, easements, and restrictions last above referred to, and with and subject to the rights and easements in said covered passage-way as they now exist: and we appraise this lot at the sum of twenty-five hundred dollars.

Lot N. All that lot of land in said Boston, with the buildings thereon, bounded southerly by the middle of Lyndeboro' Place, thirteen feet six inches; westerly by land late of J. E.

& N. Brown, by a line passing through the middle of the partition-wall, forty-five feet six inches; northerly by land late of Frederick Beck, thirteen feet six inches; and easterly by the lot of land next hereinbefore described by a line passing through the middle of a covered common passage-way and the partition-wall over the same, as they now exist, forty-five feet five and three-quarters inches. With and subject to the rights, easements, and restrictions upon which said Odin held the same, and with and subject to the rights and easements in said covered passage-way as they now exist: and we appraise this lot at the sum of twenty-five hundred dollars.

AND NOW having, as hereinbefore set forth, appraised all the real estate of which said deceased died seized in this State, which any party interested desired to have included in this partition, we find that such appraisal amounts in the aggregate to the sum of three hundred and fifty-three thousand eight hundred and eighty-nine and $\frac{58}{100}$ dollars ($353,889.58).

And we are directed by said warrant to make such partition among the devisees of said deceased (whose names and shares are therein set forth), being the same persons as named in the fourteenth article of the will of said deceased, with the exception of William White Dorr, whose contingent interest, as we are informed, never vested, by reason of his decease.

And we also find that said devisees, or some of them, have paid for and received a perpetual guaranty from the Proprietors of Forest Hills Cemetery for the perpetual maintenance and repair of the Odin tomb and lot at Forest Hills, Roxbury, in lieu of a personal maintenance and repair of the same, as directed by said will.

And said shares so to be by us divided, assigned, and set off in severalty, each amounts to one-eleventh of the aggregate appraisal aforesaid; to wit, to the sum of thirty-two thousand one hundred and seventy-one and $\frac{78}{100}$ dollars ($32,171.78).

And after having heard the parties present, and interested in the matter, and fully considered and deliberated thereupon, we proceeded to make such partition as follows:—

We divide, assign, and set off to ANNA F. ODIN of said Boston, single woman, one of said devisees named in said warrant and in said will, as and for her full eleventh part of all said real estate, to hold to her in severalty, and to her heirs and assigns forever, the lot of land on said High Street, with the buildings, conveyed to said Odin by John Homans, and hereinbefore, in the appraisal, designated as "Number two (2)," reference being had thereto for description, appraised at $14,294.50.

Also the lot of land on said Harvard Street, with the buildings, conveyed to said Odin by John O. Pettes, and hereinbefore, in the appraisal, designated as "Number seven (7)," reference being had thereto for description, appraised at $10,000.

Also the lot of land on said Allen Street, with the buildings, conveyed to said Odin by Asa and Phineas Clark, and hereinbefore, in the appraisal, designated as "Number nineteen (19)," reference being had thereto for description, appraised at $5,500.

Also the lot of land on said Lyndeboro' Place, with the buildings, hereinbefore, in the appraisal, designated as "Lot N," reference being had thereto for description, appraised at $2,500.

And the foregoing estates, assigned as aforesaid, amount in value to the sum of $32,294.50; being of greater value than the share of said Anna F. Odin by the sum of $122.72.

And we therefore award, that, for equality of partition, the said Anna F. Odin pay to William H. Webb, Trustee for Benjamin Dalton Dorr, under an indenture recorded with Suffolk Deeds lib. 911, fol. 227, the sum of fifty-four and $\frac{28}{100}$ dollars; and that she further pay, to equalize partition, unto Mary L. Currier, hereinafter named, the sum of sixty-eight and $\frac{44}{100}$ dollars.

And we divide, assign, and set off to HARRIET L. ODIN of said Boston, a minor, under the guardianship of John L. Emmons, and one of the devisees named in said warrant and in said will, as and for her full eleventh part of all said real estate, to hold to her in severalty, and to her heirs and assigns forever, the lot of land on the easterly side of said Broad Street, with the buildings, conveyed to said Odin by Nabby Joy, and hereinbefore in the appraisal designated as "Number eleven (11)," reference being had thereto for description, and subject to the lease there referred to, appraised at $15,000.

Also the lot of land on said Bulfinch Street, with the buildings, hereinbefore, in the appraisal, designated as "Lot K," reference being had thereto for description, and other easements and provisions, and subject to the lease there mentioned, appraised at $17,000.

And the foregoing estates, assigned as aforesaid, amount in value to the sum of $32,000; being of less value than the share of said Harriet L. Odin by the sum of $171.78.

And we therefore award, that, for equality of partition, the said Harriet L. receive from George O. Currier and Charles H. Richardson, as they are trustees under the deed recorded with Suffolk Deeds, lib. 932, fol. 253, the sum of $171.78.

And we divide, assign, and set off to MARY W. D. SCHAFFER of Philadelphia, in the State of Pennsylvania, widow, and one of the devisees named in said warrant and in said will, as and for her full eleventh part of all said real estate, to hold to her in severalty, and to her heirs and assigns forever, one undivided half of the lot of land on said High Street, with the buildings thereon, hereinbefore in the appraisal designated as "Lot A," reference being had thereto for description, subject to the stipulations and agreements hereinbefore set forth as to betterments, easements, and partition-walls (she, said Mary W. D., having consented to hold the same in common and undivided with Harriet O. Carpenter, wife of J. Edward Carpenter), appraised at $15,139.58.

Also all that lot of land on said Bulfinch Street, and at the corner of said Howard Street, with the buildings, hereinbefore in the appraisal designated as "Lot G," reference being had thereto for description, subject to the easements and provisions there set forth, appraised at $12,500.

Also all that lot of land on said Castle Street, with the buildings, conveyed to said Odin by Maria E. Winslow and another, and hereinbefore in the appraisal designated as "Number four (4)," reference being had thereto for description, appraised at $4,500.

And the foregoing estates, assigned as aforesaid, amount in value to the sum of $32,139.58, being of less value than the share of said Mary W. D. Schaffer by the sum of $32.20.

And we therefore award, that, for equality of partition, the said Mary W. D. Schaffer receive from Harriet W. Currier, or her guardian, the sum of $32.20.

And we divide, assign, and set off to ESTHER O. D. WEBB, wife of William H. Webb of said Philadelphia, in her right, as one of the devisees named in said warrant and will, as and for her full eleventh part of all said real estate, to hold to her in severalty, and to her heirs and assigns forever, one undivided half of the lot of land on said High Street, with the buildings, hereinbefore in the appraisal designated as "Lot C," reference being had thereto for description, subject to the stipulations hereinbefore set forth as to betterments, easements, and partition-walls (she, said Esther O. D., having consented to hold the same in common and undivided with

William H. Webb as trustee for Benjamin Dalton Dorr, under a deed recorded with Suffolk Deeds, lib. 911, fol. 227, and with said Benjamin Dalton Dorr, so far as his rights are not devested by the last deed aforesaid), appraised at $15,617.50.

Also all that lot of land on said Pinckney Street, with the buildings, hereinbefore in the appraisal designated as "Lot D," reference being had thereto for description, and subject as there referred to, appraised at $8,500.

Also all that lot of land on said McLean Street, with the buildings hereinbefore in the appraisal designated as "Number seventeen (17)," reference being had thereto for description, subject as there expressed, appraised at $8,000.

And the foregoing estates, assigned as aforesaid, amount in value to the sum of $32,117.50; being of less value than the share of said Esther O. D. Webb by the sum of $54.28.

And we therefore award, that, for equality of partition, the said Esther O. D. Webb receive from George O. Currier the sum of $54.28.

And we divide, assign, and set off to HARRIET O. CARPENTER, wife of J. Edward Carpenter of said Philadelphia, in her right, as one of the devisees named in said warrant and will, and as and for her full eleventh part of all said real estate, to hold to her in severalty, and to her heirs and assigns forever, one undivided half of the lot of land on said High Street, with the buildings, hereinbefore in the appraisal designated as "Lot A," reference being had thereto for description, subject to the stipulations and agreements hereinbefore set forth as to betterments, easements, and partition-walls (she, said Harriet O., having consented to hold the same in common and undivided with Mary W. D. Schaffer), appraised at $15,139.59.

Also all that lot of land on said Bulfinch Street, with the buildings, hereinbefore in the appraisal designated as "Lot H," reference being had thereto for description, subject to the easements and provisions there set forth, appraised at $10,000.

Also all that lot of land on said Pinckney Street, with the buildings hereinbefore in the appraisal designated as "Lot E," reference being had thereto for description, and subject as there referred to, appraised at $7,000.

And the foregoing estates, assigned as aforesaid, amount in value to the sum of $32,139.59; being of less value than the share of said Harriet O. Carpenter by the sum of 32.19.

And we therefore award, that, for equality of partition, the said Harriet O. Carpenter receive from Harriet W. Currier, or her guardian, the sum of $32.19.

And we divide, assign, and set off to WILLIAM HEWITT WEBB, Trustee for BENJAMIN DALTON DORR, under and by virtue of a deed dated Oct. 1, 1867, and recorded with Suffolk Deeds, lib. 911, fol. 227, but upon the trusts set forth in said deed; and to said BENJAMIN DALTON DORR, one of said devisees, the reversionary interest in the trust estate, as and for his full eleventh part of all said real estate, to hold in severalty to said trustee for life, unless previously revoked, upon the trusts set forth in said deed, and to hold the reversionary interest to said Benjamin Dalton Dorr, and his heirs and assigns forever, one undivided half of the lot of land on said High Street, with the buildings, hereinbefore in the appraisal designated as "Lot C," reference being had thereto for description, subject to the stipulations hereinbefore set forth as to betterments, easements, and partition-walls (said trustee, and said Benjamin Dalton Dorr, having consented to hold the same in common and undivided with said Esther O. D. Webb), appraised at $15,617.50.

Also all that lot of land on said Bulfinch Street, with the buildings, hereinbefore in the appraisal designated as "Lot L," reference being had thereto for description, with and subject to the easements, provisions, and leases as there mentioned, appraised at $10,000.

Also all that lot of land on said Kneeland Place, with the buildings, hereinbefore in the appraisal designated as "Number eight (8)," reference being had thereto for description, subject as there mentioned, appraised at $6,500.

And the foregoing estates assigned as aforesaid amount in value to the sum of $32,117.50, being of less value than the share of said trustee by the sum of $54.28.

And we therefore award, that, for equality of partition, the said trustee receive from Anna F. Odin the sum of $54.28.

And we divide, assign, and set off to GEORGE O. CURRIER and CHARLES H. RICHARDSON, as they are Trustees for AMELIA O. RICHARDSON, wife of Joseph Richardson, under and by virtue of a deed dated July 10, 1868, and recorded with Suffolk Deeds lib. 932, fol. 253 (said Amelia being one of said devisees), and for their full eleventh part of all said real estate, to hold in severalty to said trustees in fee simple, but upon the trusts set forth in said deed, all that lot of land on said Carver Street, with the buildings, conveyed to said George Odin by Samuel F. Towle, and hereinbefore in the appraisal designated as "Number six (6)," reference being had thereto for description, appraised at $6,000.

Also all that lot of land on said Somerset Street, with the buildings, conveyed to said George Odin by James Dennie, and hereinbefore in the appraisal designated as "Number fifteen (15)," reference being had thereto for description, with and subject to the terms and provisions there mentioned, appraised at $16,500.

Also all that lot of land on said Howard Street, with the buildings, hereinbefore in the appraisal designated as "Lot F," reference being had thereto for description, with and subject to the easements and provisions there mentioned, appraised at $10,000.

And the foregoing estates assigned as aforesaid amount in value to the sum of $32,500, being of greater value than the share of said trustees by the sum of $328.22.

And we therefore award, that, for equality of partition, the said trustees pay to Mary L. Currier the sum of $156.44; and that they further pay, to equalize partition, unto Harriet L. Odin, or her guardian, the sum of $171.78.

And we divide, assign, and set off to GEORGE O. CURRIER of West Roxbury, as one of said devisees, as and for his full eleventh part of all said real estate, to hold to him in severalty and to his heirs and assigns forever, one undivided half of the lot of land on said High Street, with the buildings, hereinbefore in the appraisal designated as "Lot B," reference being had thereto for description, subject to the stipulations hereinbefore set forth as to betterments, easements, and partition-walls (he, said George O., having consented to hold the same in common and undivided with Harriet W. Currier), appraised at $14,240.41.

Also all that lot of land on said Bulfinch Street, with the buildings, hereinbefore in the appraisal designated as "Lot J," reference being had thereto for description, subject to the provisions, stipulations, and lease there mentioned, appraised at $9,000.

Also all that lot of land in said Chelsea, with the buildings, hereinbefore in the appraisal designated as "Number twenty (20)," reference being had thereto for description, appraised at $5,000.

Also all that lot of land on said Suffolk Street, with the buildings thereon, conveyed to said George Odin by Henry W. Walker, hereinbefore in the appraisal designated as "Number three (3)", reference being had thereto for description, appraised at $4,000.

And the foregoing estates, assigned as aforesaid, amount in value to the sum of $32,240.41, being of greater value than the share of said George O. by the sum of $68.63.

And we therefore award, that, for equality of partition, the said George O. Currier pay to said Esther O. D. Webb the sum of $54.28; and that he further pay to Mary L. Currier, to equalize partition, the sum of $14.35.

And we divide, assign, and set off to MARY L. CURRIER of West Roxbury, single woman, one of said devisees, as and for her full eleventh part of all said real estate, to hold to her in severalty and to her heirs and assigns forever, all that lot of land on said Chauncy Street, with the buildings, conveyed to said George Odin by William A. Swift et al., and hereinbefore in the appraisal designated as "Number nine (9)," reference being had thereto for description, with the rights and easements belonging, appraised at $18,000.

Also all that lot of land on said Pleasant Street, with the buildings, conveyed to said George Odin by George Parkman, and hereinbefore in the appraisal designated as "Number five (5)," reference being had thereto for description, appraised at $10,928.30.

Also all that lot of land on said Wendell Street, with the buildings, conveyed to said George Odin by Robert Briggs, hereinbefore in the appraisal designated as "Number ten (10)," reference being had thereto for description, appraised at $3,000.

And the foregoing estates, assigned as aforesaid, amount in value to the sum of $31,928.30, being of less value than the share of said Mary L. Currier by the sum of $243.48.

And we therefore award, that, for equality of partition, the said Mary L. Currier receive of Harriet W. Currier, or her guardian, the sum of $4.25; and that she further receive of George O. Currier the sum of $14.35; and that she further receive of Anna F. Odin the sum of $68.44; and that she further receive of the trustees aforesaid, for said Amelia O. Richardson, the sum of $156.44.

And we divide, assign, and set off to HARRIET W. CURRIER of West Roxbury, a minor under the guardianship of Benjamin H. Currier, and one of said devisees, as and for her full eleventh part of all said real estate, to hold to her in severalty, and to her heirs and assigns forever, one undivided half of the lot of land on said High Street, with the buildings, hereinbefore in the appraisal designated as "Lot B," reference being had thereto for description, subject to the stipulations hereinbefore set forth as to betterments, easements, and partition-walls (she, said Harriet W., having, by her said guardian, consented to hold the same in common and undivided with said George O. Currier), appraised at $14,240.42.

Also all that lot of land on said Bulfinch Street, with the buildings, hereinbefore in the appraisal designated as "Lot I," reference being had thereto for description, with and subject to the provisions and stipulations there mentioned, appraised at $9,500.

Also all that lot of land on said McLean Street, with the buildings, hereinbefore in the appraisal designated as "Number eighteen (18)," reference being had thereto for description, subject as there expressed, appraised at $8,500.

And the foregoing estates, assigned as aforesaid, amount in value to the sum of $32,240.42, being of greater value than the share of said Harriet W. Currier by the sum of $68.64.

And we therefore award, that, for equality of partition, the said Harriet W. Currier, by her guardian aforesaid, pay to said Mary W. D. Schaffer the sum of $32.20, and further pay to said Harriet O. Carpenter the sum of $32.19, and further pay to said Mary L. Currier the sum of $4.25.

And finally we divide, assign, and set off to HARRIET W. O. KELLOGG, wife of Day O. Kellogg of Brooklyn, in the State of New York, one of said devisees, as and for her full eleventh part of all said real estate, to hold in severalty to her use during her natural life [and at her decease to be equally divided among such of the other devisees aforesaid as shall then be living and their heirs forever], all that lot of land on the westerly side of said Broad Street, with the buildings, conveyed to said George Odin by Samuel Sanford, and hereinbefore in the appraisal designated as "Number twelve (12)," reference being had thereto for description, with all the easements and privileges belonging, appraised at $18,671.78.

Also the lot of land on said Lyndeboro' Place, with the buildings, hereinbefore in the appraisal designated as "Lot M," reference being had thereto for description, appraised at $2,500.

Also all that lot of land on said Bulfinch Street, with the buildings, conveyed to said George Odin by Thomas Crehore, and hereinbefore in the appraisal designated as "Number sixteen (16)," reference being had thereto, and subject as there set forth, for full description appraised at $11,000.

And the foregoing estates, assigned as aforesaid to the said Harriet W. O. Kellogg for her natural life, amount in value to the sum of $32,171.78, being one full equal share, and no more.

And we have now appraised and divided all the real estate by said warrant directed, and in conformity therewith; and, believing the same to do justice and equity to all parties interested, return the same to the Honorable Probate Court for acceptance and approval.

} *Commissioners.*

I, John Goldsbury, of Boston, appointed by the Judge of Probate Court for the County of Suffolk to appear and act as the next friend of all such persons not in being at the time of application for the foregoing partition, as might be interested, either under the devise to Harriet W. O. Kellogg for life, with contingent remainder over, under the fourteenth article of the will of George Odin, or under any of the provisions or contingencies of the deed of Benjamin Dalton Dorr to William Hewett Webb, trustee, or under any of the provisions or contingencies of the deed of Joseph Richardson and Amelia O. Richardson to George O. Currier and Charles H. Richardson, trustees, both of which deeds are referred to in said foregoing partition, do hereby accept of such appointment, and believing said partition to be for the interest of all such persons not in being as aforesaid, do, as such next friend of all such persons, assent to said foregoing partition, and request the same may be confirmed without further notice.

We, the undersigned, being all the persons interested in the foregoing Report, hereby assent thereto, and request that the same be confirmed without further notice; and we to whom money is awarded thereby to equalize the partition acknowledge the receipt thereof; and we to whom any estates have, by the foregoing Report, been assigned to hold together in common, do hereby accept of and approve such assignment; and, furthermore, in ratification and approval of all the same, and to effect a confirmatory division of all said real estate, we, the undersigned, other than the said Anna F. Odin, hereby release, and confirm to said Anna F. and her heirs and assigns, all the real estate by the foregoing Report assigned and set off to her.

And we, the undersigned, other than said Harriet L. Odin, hereby release and confirm to said Harriet L., and her heirs and assigns, all the real estate by the foregoing Report assigned and set off to her.

And we, the undersigned, other than the said Mary W. D. Schaffer, hereby release and confirm to said Mary W. D., and her heirs and assigns, all the real estate by the foregoing Re port assigned and set off to her.

And we, the undersigned, other than the said Esther O. D. Webb, hereby release and confirm to said Esther O. D., and her heirs and assigns, all the real estate by the foregoing Report assigned and set off to her.

And we, the undersigned, other than the said Harriet O. Carpenter, hereby release and confirm to said Harriet O., and her heirs and assigns, all the real estate by the foregoing Report assigned and set off to her.

And we, the undersigned, other than the said William H. Webb, as trustee for Benjamin Dalton Dorr, and other than said Benjamin Dalton Dorr, hereby release and confirm to said trustee, for life, upon the trusts hereinbefore referred to, all the real estate by the foregoing Report assigned and set off to him, and release and confirm to said Benjamin Dalton Dorr, and his heirs and assigns, all the reversionary interest in the same.

And we, the undersigned, other than the said George O. Currier and Charles H. Richardson, as they are trustees for Amelia O. Richardson, hereby release and confirm to said George O. and Charles H., and their heirs and assigns as such trustees, upon the trusts in the deed to them set forth, all the real estate by the foregoing Report assigned and set off to them.

And we, the undersigned, other than said George O. Currier, in his own right, hereby release and confirm to said George O., and his heirs and assigns, all the real estate by the foregoing Report assigned and set off to him in his own right.

And we, the undersigned, other than said Mary L. Currier, hereby release and confirm to said Mary L., and her heirs and assigns, all the real estate by the foregoing Report assigned and set off to her.

And we, the undersigned, other than the said Harriet W. Currier, hereby release and confirm to said Harriet W., and her heirs and assigns, all the real estate by the foregoing Report assigned and set off to her.

And we, the undersigned, other than the said Harriet W. O. Kellogg, hereby release and confirm to the said Harriet W. O. Kellogg, for the term of her natural life, all the real estate by the foregoing report assigned and set off to her.

In witness whereof, we have hereto set our hands and seals, this
A. D. 1868.

SUFFOLK, ss. At a Probate Court holden at Boston, in said County of Suffolk, on the day of A. D. 186

The foregoing Report having been examined and considered, and all parties interested having been notified, and had an opportunity to be heard thereon before this Court, and having assented thereto in writing, and it appearing that said Commissioners were sworn according to law, and gave notice, as ordered by Court, that said partition has been properly made, and that all the money therein awarded has been paid or secured: —

It is DECREED that said Report be accepted, and the partition confirmed and established, and that the premises be assigned as described, and set off to the several parties therein named.

Judge of Probate Court.

GENERAL SCHEDULE.

No. 1.		Estates 43, 45, 47, 49, and 51 High Street, also " 32, 34, and 36 Purchase Street, divided into three lots:		
	Lot A.	One half to Mary W. D. Schaffer,	$15,139.58	
		The other half to Harriet O. Carpenter,	15,139.59	$30,279.17
	Lot B.	One half to Harriet W. Currier,	14,240.42	
		The other half to George O. Currier,	14,240.41	28,480.83
	Lot C.	One half to Esther O. D. Webb,	15,617.50	
		The other half to W. H. Webb, trus. for B. Dalton Dorr,	15,617.50	31,235.
No. 2.		Estate numbered 33 High Street to Anna F. Odin,		14,294.50
" **3.**		" " 9 Suffolk Street to George O. Currier,		4,000.
" **4.**		" " 62 Castle Street to Mary W. D. Schaffer,		4,500.
" **5.**		" " 18 and 20 Pleasant Street to Mary L. Currier,		10,928.30
" **6.**		" " 36 Carver St. to trus. of Amelia O. Richardson,		6,000.
" **7.**		" " 16 Harvard Street to Anna F. Odin,		10,000.
" **8.**		" " 5 Kneeland Place to W. H. Webb, trustee for B. Dalton Dorr,		6,500.
" **9.**		" " 59 Chauncy Street to Mary L. Currier,		18,000.
" **10.**		" " 4 Wendell Street to Mary L. Currier,		3,000.
" **11.**		" " 54 and 56 Broad Street to Harriet L. Odin,		15,000.
" **12.**		" " 69 Broad Street to Harriet W. O. Kellogg,		18,671.78
" **13.**	**Lot D.**	" " 4 Pinckney Street to Esther O. D. Webb,		8,500.
	" **E.**	" " 6 and 8 Pinckney Street to Harriet O. Carpenter,		7,000.
" **14.**	" **F.**	" " 52 Howard St. to trus. of Amelia O. Richardson,		10,000.
	" **G.**	" " 12 Bulfinch Street to Mary W. D. Schaffer,		12,500.
	" **H.**	" " 14 " " to Harriet O. Carpenter,		10,000.
	" **I.**	" " 16 " " to Harriet W. Currier,		9,500.
	" **J.**	" " 18 " " to George O. Currier,		9,000.
	" **K.**	" " 20 " " to Harriet L. Odin,		17,000.
	" **L.**	" " 22 " " to W. H. Webb, tr. B. D. Dorr,		10,000.
No. 15.		" " 24 Somerset Street, trus. of Amelia O. Richardson,		16,500.
" **16.**		" " 7 Bulfinch Street, to Harriet W. O. Kellogg,		11.000.
" **17.**		" " 21 McLean Street, to Esther O. D. Webb,		8,000.
" **18.**		" " 22 " " to Harriet W. Currier,		8,500.
" **19.**		" " 28 Allen Street, to Anna F. Odin,		5,500.
" **20.**		" " — in Chelsea, to George O. Currier,		5.000.
" **21.**	**Lot M.**	" " 2 Lyndeboro Place, to Anna F. Odin,		2.500.
	" **N.**	" " 4 " " to Harriet W. O. Kellogg,		2,500.
				$353,889.58
		One eleventh of the above is equal to		$32,171.78

CLASSIFIED SCHEDULE.

Anna F. Odin.

No. 2.	Estate 33 High Street,	$14,294.50
No. 7.	" 16 Harvard Street,	10,000.00
No. 19.	" 28 Allen Street,	5,500.00
Lot N.	" 2 Lyndeboro Place,	2,500.00
		$32,294.50
	To pay W. H. Webb, tr., $54.28 ; and Mary L. Currier, $68.44,	122.72
		$32,171.78

Harriet L. Odin, Minor.

No. 11.	Estate 54 and 56 Broad Street,	$15,000.00
Lot K.	" 20 Bulfinch Street,	17,000.00
	To receive from trustees of Amelia O. Richardson,	171.78
		$32,171.78

Mary W. D. Schaffer.

Lot A.	High and Purchase Street, an undivided half of this lot,	$15,139.58
Lot G.	Estate 12 Bulfinch Street,	12,500.00
No. 4.	" on Castle Street,	4,500.00
	To receive from Harriet W. Currier,	32.20
		$32,171.78

Esther O. D. Webb.

Lot C.	High and Purchase Street, an undivided half of this lot,	$15,617.50
Lot D.	Estate 4 Pinckney Street,	8,500.00
No. 17.	" 21 McLean Street,	8,000.00
	To receive from Geo O. Currier,	54.28
		$32,171.78

Harriet O. Carpenter.

Lot A.	High and Purchase Street, an undivided half of this lot,	$15,139.59
Lot H.	Estate 14 Bulfinch Street,	10,000.00
Lot E.	" 8 and 6 Pinckney Street,	7,000.00
	To receive from Harriet W. Currier,	32.19
		$32,171.78

W. H. Webb, Trustee of B. Dalton Dorr.

Lot C.	High and Purchase Street, an undivided half of this lot,	$15,617.50
Lot L.	Estate 22 Bulfinch Street,	10,000.00
No. 8.	" Kneeland Place,	6,500.00
	To receive from Anna F. Odin,	54.28
		$32,171.78

Trustees of Amelia O. Richardson.

No. 6.	Estate 36 Carver Street,	$ 6,000.00
No. 15.	" Somerset Street,	16,500.00
Lot F.	" Howard Street,	10,000.00
		32.500.00
	To pay Mary L. Currier, $156.44; Harriet L. Odin, $171.78,	328.22
		$32,171.78

George O. Currier.

Lot B.	High and Purchase Street, an undivided half of this lot,	$14,240.41
Lot J.	Estate 18 Bulfinch Street,	9,000.00
No. 3.	" Suffolk Street,	4,000.00
No. 20.	" at Chelsea,	5,000.00
		$32,240.41
	To pay Esther O. D. Webb, $54.28; and Mary L. Currier, $14.35,	68.63
		$32,171,78

Mary L. Currier.

No. 9.	Estate 59 Chauncy Street,	$18,000.00
No. 5.	" Pleasant Street,	10,928.30
No. 10.	" Wendell Street,	3,000.00
	To receive from Harriet W. Currier, $4.25; George O Currier, $14.35; Anna F. Odin, $68.44; and Trustees of Amelia O. Richardson, $156.44,	243.48
		$32,171.78

Harriet W. Currier, Minor.

Lot B.	High and Purchase Street, an undivided half of this lot,	$14,240.42
Lot I.	Estate 16 Bulfinch Street,	9,500.00
No. 18.	" 22 McLean Street,	8,500.00
		32,240.42
	To pay M. W. D. Schaffer, $32.20; H. O. Carpenter, $32.19; Mary L. Currier, $4.25,	68.64
		$32,171.78

Harriet W. O. Kellogg.

No. 12.	Estate 69 Broad Street,	$18,671,78
No. 16.	" 7 Bulfinch Place,	11,000.00
Lot M.	" 4 Lyndeboro Place,	2,500.00
		$32,171.78

www.ingramcontent.com/pod-product-compliance
Lightning Source LLC
LaVergne TN
LVHW011141110826
845150LV00008B/2451